COMMUNITY HELPERS

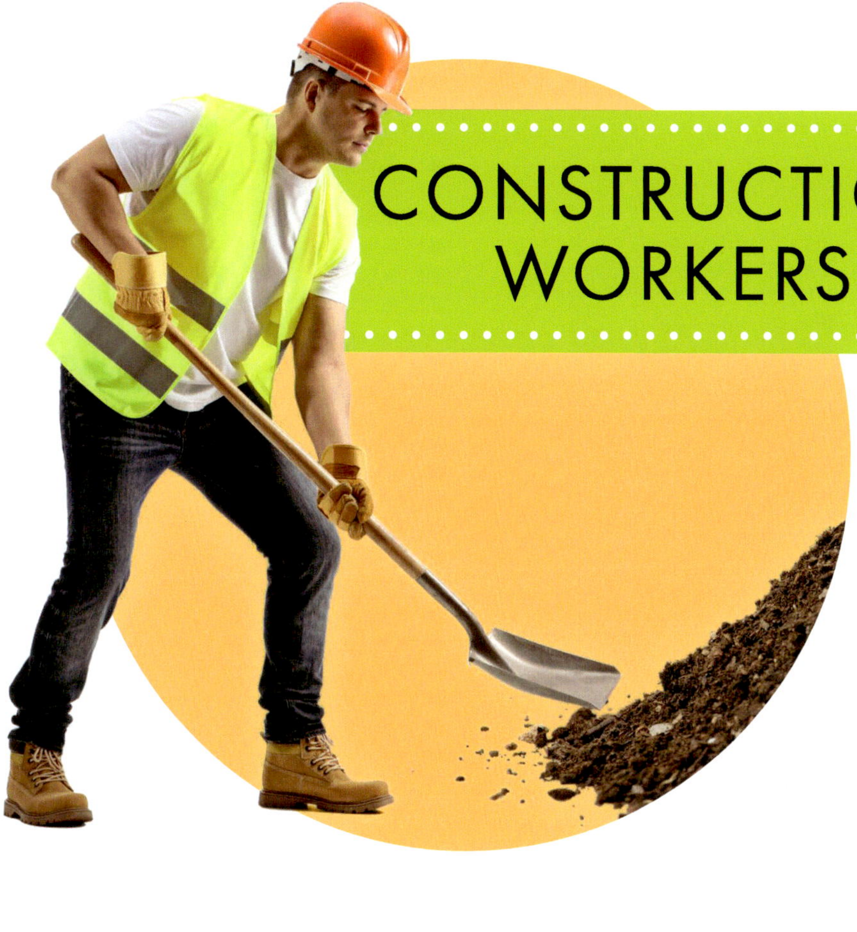

CONSTRUCTION WORKERS

by Golriz Golkar

hard hat

crane

Look for these words and pictures as you read.

digger

cement

Construction workers help us.
What do they do?

hard hat

They put on a hard hat and boots.
They wear a vest.
It is time for work!

Beep! Beep!
A worker uses a crane.
It swings a big ball.
Boom! Down goes a wall!

crane

digger

Here comes a digger.
One worker digs a hole.

EURO SCAVI
BUSCEMA

He mixes some cement.

He smooths it out.

The road is fixed.

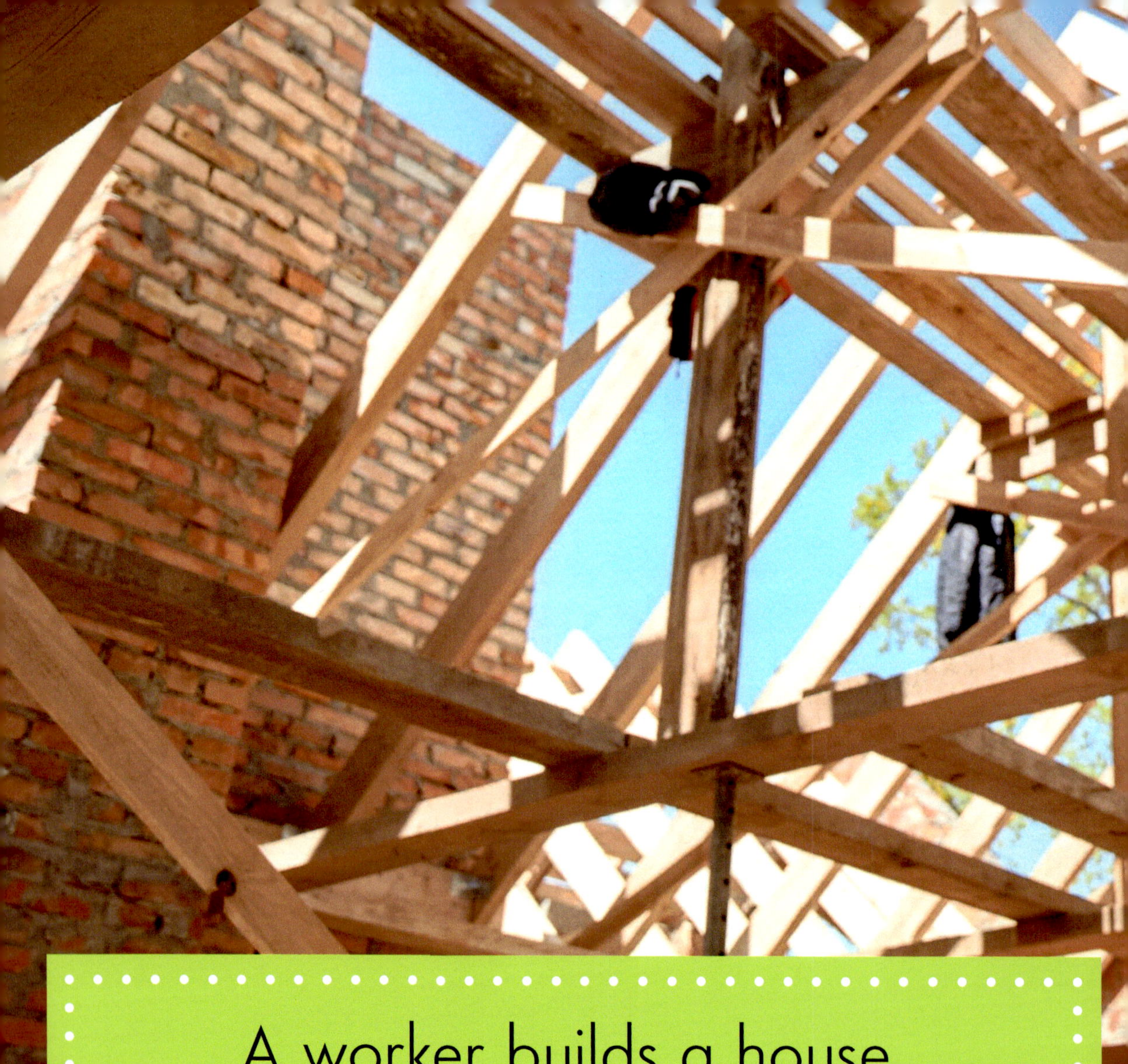

A worker builds a house.
She makes sure the wood is strong.
A family will live here.

Construction workers build our towns. Their work keeps us safe and sound!

hard hat

crane

Did you find?

digger

cement

Spot is published by Amicus Learning, an imprint of Amicus
P.O. Box 227, Mankato, MN 56002
www.amicuspublishing.us

Library of Congress Cataloging-in-Publication Data
Names: Golkar, Golriz, author.
Title: Construction workers / by Golriz Golkar.
Description: Mankato, MN : Amicus Learning, an imprint of Amicus, [2026] | Series: Spot community helpers | Audience term: Children | Audience: Ages 4–7 | Audience: Grades K–1 | Summary: "Construction workers build buildings, roads, bridges, and more. Learn how they help the community in this low-level beginning reader that reinforces new vocabulary with a search-and-find feature. A great early social studies book that will inspire kindergartners and first graders to learn about jobs in their community"— Provided by publisher.
Identifiers: LCCN 2024043689 (print) | LCCN 2024043690 (ebook) | ISBN 9798892004879 (library binding) | ISBN 9798892005418 (paperback) | ISBN 9798892005951 (ebook)
Subjects: LCSH: Construction workers—Juvenile literature. | Occupations—Juvenile literature.
Classification: LCC HD8039.B89 G65 2026 (print) | LCC HD8039.B89 (ebook) | DDC 331.7/624—dc23/eng/20250105
LC record available at https://lccn.loc.gov/2024043689
LC ebook record available at https://lccn.loc.gov/2024043690

Ana Brauer, editor
Deb Miner, series designer
Sara Hood, book designer and photo researcher

Photos by Alamy Stock Photo/Martin Bond, 6–7; Shutterstock/Angelo Giampiccolo, 10–11, BigPixel Photo, 3, Dusan Petkovic, 8–9, FREEPIK2, 5, hugo_34, 14, Ljupco Smokovski, 1, M2020, cover, YAKOBCHUK VIACHESLAV, 12–13